T0182558

A TASTE OF

Disney

Snacks

A TASTE OF

Snacks

Bite-Size Recipes
in a Snack-Size Book

INSIGHT EDITIONS

SAN RAFAEL · LOS ANGELES · LONDON

Contents

DIETARY KEY

GF: Gluten-free
GF*: Easily Made Gluten-free
V: Vegetarian

V+: Vegan
V+*: Easily Made Vegan

Introduction

Welcome to *A Taste of Disney: Snacks*, a selection of delicious recipes inspired by beloved Disney films. From the creature comforts of Mouse-approved Cheesy Corn Puffs and the Cave of Wonders Cardamom Breadsticks to the chompable delights of White Rabbit's Garden Crudité and Mexican Chocolate Popcorn, you can prepare snacks for yourself, family, and friends. Gather round, dig in, and taste your way into celebrating your love of Disney characters and films. Enjoy!

Chicken Schnitzel Bites

Snow White and the Seven Dwarfs

In the forest, after being spared by the Queen's Huntsman, Snow White takes up residence with the Seven and lovingly prepares meals to serve these hard-working miners. After a full day, the Friends would surely look forward to a meal like schnitzel—thinly pounded chicken that's breaded and fried crispy—especially with a dash of freshly squeezed lemon juice.

Chicken Schnitzel Bites

Yield: About 16 schnitzel bites

1 pound chicken breasts (about 2 breasts)
1 cup all-purpose flour
1 teaspoon salt, plus a pinch
1 teaspoon freshly ground black pepper, plus a pinch
1 large egg
¼ teaspoon dry mustard
1 cup panko breadcrumbs
¼ cup canola oil
1 tablespoon chopped fresh parsley
1 lemon, cut into 8 wedges

1. Pound each chicken breast to ¼-inch thickness. Cut each breast into 8 pieces.

2. Sift the flour, the 1 teaspoon salt, and the 1 teaspoon pepper onto a plate.

3. Combine the egg, dry mustard, and a pinch each of salt and pepper in a small bowl; whisk thoroughly to combine.

4. Place the breadcrumbs on a second plate.

5. Coat each piece of chicken first in flour, then in the egg mixture, then in breadcrumbs. Set each piece on a plate.

6. Line a plate with paper towels; set aside. Heat the oil in a large skillet over medium heat. Add the chicken in a single layer to the pan. Cook for 2 to 3 minutes, turn, and cook another 2 to 3 minutes, or until golden and cooked through. Transfer to the towel-lined plate.

7. Sprinkle the chicken with parsley and serve with lemon wedges. Direct guests to squeeze the lemon onto the schnitzel.

Wild Chase Tea Biscuits

The Adventures of Ichabod and Mr. Toad

Mr. Toad is always on the go, racing from one place to another. But that doesn't mean he's not willing to stop for a tasty treat. These fabulous biscuits might give him a reason to stop. With such delicious biscuits and homemade strawberry jam, your friends will be sticking around for a while, too!

Wild Chase Tea Biscuits

V | **Yield:** 2 dozen (2-inch) biscuits and 5 half-pints jam

STRAWBERRY FREEZER JAM
8 cups fresh ripe whole strawberries, hulled, divided
1⅔ cups granulated sugar
5 teaspoons instant powdered fruit pectin
1 tablespoon lemon zest

BISCUITS
1½ cups all-purpose flour
½ cup granulated sugar
¼ teaspoon salt
⅛ teaspoon ground cardamom
½ cup cold butter, cut up
1 egg
¼ cup dried currants or chopped
dried cherries
1 tablespoon orange zest
Granulated sugar or sparkling sanding sugar (optional)

1. **To make the jam:** In a large bowl, crush 1 cup of the strawberries with a potato masher. Continue adding berries, 1 cup at a time, crushing them, until you have 4 cups crushed berries.

2. In a very large bowl, stir together the sugar and fruit pectin. Add the crushed berries and lemon zest. Stir for 3 minutes. Ladle into half-pint freezer containers, leaving ½ inch of headspace at the top. Let stand at room temperature for 30 minutes. Freeze for up to 1 year. Once jam is opened, store in the refrigerator for up to 3 weeks.

3. **To make the biscuits:** Heat the oven to 350°F.

4. In a food processor bowl, combine the flour, sugar, salt, and cardamom. Process until combined. Add the butter pieces. Pulse until the butter is the size of coarse crumbs. Add the egg, currants, and orange zest. Process until combined and dough begins to form a ball in the food processor. If the dough is sticky, wrap in plastic wrap and chill in the refrigerator for 1 to 2 hours.

5. Line a large rimmed baking pan with parchment paper. On a lightly floured surface, roll the dough out to ¼-inch thickness. Cut out the dough with a round 2-inch biscuit cutter. Place biscuits 1 inch apart on the prepared pan. Sprinkle the tops with additional granulated sugar, if desired.

6. Bake until bottoms are lightly browned, 8 to 10 minutes. Serve warm with jam.

Mouse-approved Cheesy Corn Puffs

Cinderella

Cinderella starts almost every morning scattering corn in the yard for the animals. For the chickens, it's just breakfast, but for Cinderella's mouse friend Gus, it's a special treat—a fact he makes known by gathering up as many kernels as his little arms can carry! This irresistible cheesy corn puff would make a treat even more special for Gus.

Mouse-approved Cheesy Corn Puffs

V | Yield: About 4 dozen puffs

1 cup water
¼ cup butter
½ teaspoon salt
Pinch cayenne pepper
1 cup all-purpose flour
4 large eggs
1 cup shredded sharp
cheddar cheese
¼ cup fresh or frozen
corn kernels, thawed
¼ cup grated
Parmesan cheese
1 tablespoon
yellow cornmeal

1. Heat the oven to 425°F. Adjust the racks to the center of oven. Line two large baking sheets with parchment paper.

2. In a large saucepan, bring the water, butter, salt, and cayenne to a boil over medium heat. Add the flour all at once. Stir with a wooden spoon until a smooth ball forms. Remove from heat and let stand for 5 minutes. Add the eggs, one at a time, beating with an electric mixer after each addition until smooth. Stir in the cheddar cheese and corn.

3. Using two spoons or a small cookie scoop, drop dough into 1-inch balls, 1 inch apart, on the prepared baking sheets. Sprinkle the tops of the balls with the Parmesan cheese and cornmeal.

4. Bake until golden brown, 20 to 25 minutes. Serve warm.

White Rabbit's Garden Crudité

Alice in Wonderland

The White Rabbit has the lushest vegetable garden, and he is quite proud of it. His little patch of paradise is sprinkled with carrots, turnips, and delightfully fresh cucumbers. If your own garden offers up such a bounty, a vegetable crudité makes for a sensible— and salubrious!—use of excess resources. And isn't it nice when something makes sense for a change?

White Rabbit's Garden Crudité

GF, V | **Yield:** 15 to 20 servings

1 to 2 bunches thin asparagus

2 English cucumbers

2 bunches small radishes

2 bunches baby carrots, with greens intact

20 to 30 sugar snap peas

8 ounces cream cheese, softened

2 ounces crème fraîche

1 teaspoon finely minced fresh chives

½ teaspoon finely minced fresh thyme

¼ teaspoon finely minced fresh rosemary

1. **To prepare the vegetables:** Start by blanching the asparagus. Snap off the tough ends of each stalk of asparagus. Fill a large pot with water, and bring to a boil over high heat. While the water is coming to a boil, fill a large bowl with cold water and ice, and have it standing by. When the water is boiling, put all the asparagus in at once, and boil for 1 minute. Remove the asparagus stalks with tongs, and immediately plunge them into the ice bath. Use the tongs to gently remove the stalks from the ice bath, and let them drain in a colander. Set aside.

2. Slice the cucumbers into ¼-inch slices. Slice the radishes into ¼-inch slices, leaving a few very small ones whole for garnish. Trim the carrot greens so that you have just a short bunch of stems, with few to no leaves. Gently peel. Remove the stem end and string from each sugar snap pod and split in half.

3. In a medium bowl, thoroughly mix together the cream cheese and crème fraîche.

4. Add minced chives, thyme, and rosemary, and stir until evenly distributed. Set aside.

5. Arrange the asparagus, cucumbers, radishes, carrots, and peas in neat garden rows on one or more serving platters; pat them dry, if necessary.

6. Load the cream cheese mixture into a piping bag fitted with a coupler, and have several tips standing by (such as a large petal, an open star, and a closed star). Pipe the mixture onto the vegetables, switching up the tips to add variety. If you do not have a piping bag and tips, you can spread the cream cheese mixture onto the veggies or pipe it using a sealable plastic bag with a corner snipped off.

7. Either serve immediately or refrigerate for up to 2 hours.

"Whether Pigs Have Wings" Pastries

Alice in Wonderland

The time has come to talk of whether pigs have wings. Flying pigs have never been seen, but that need not suggest that they don't exist. Perhaps this particular breed is simply good at hiding! Diners will delight in this clever twist on a childhood favorite, which tucks our storied pigs beneath a deliciously doughy blanket. What a fantastical meal!

"Whether Pigs Have Wings" Pastries

Yield: About 24 pigs in a blanket

1 cup brown sugar

1 teaspoon paprika

1 teaspoon cumin

1 teaspoon freshly ground black pepper

1 pound bacon

One 17-ounce box puff pastry, defrosted according to package directions

24 mini cocktail sausages

SPECIALTY TOOLS

1 rimmed baking sheet fitted with a baking rack

Foil

1. Preheat the oven to 375°F. Cover the baking rack with foil, and place it onto the baking sheet. With a butter knife, poke holes in rows all along the foil, to allow the bacon fat to drain onto the baking sheet. Set aside.

2. In a large bowl, mix together the sugar, paprika, cumin, and black pepper. Add the strips of bacon, and toss to coat. Place the strips of bacon onto the foil-lined rack in a single layer, and bake for 10 minutes. Remove the bacon from the oven, and allow the strips to cool while you wrap the pigs.

3. Cut each sheet of puff pastry into three equal parts. Cut each one of these sections into four strips. Wrap each mini hot dog in a strip of puff pastry, and press gently to close.

4. Cut each strip of bacon in half, and lay it over the top of each puff pastry bundle; secure it with a toothpick through both sides. Two "wings" of bacon should rest on either side of the bundle, lying flat against the baking rack.

5. Return the pastries to the oven, and bake for an additional 15 minutes or until they are golden.

6. Allow to cool for 5 minutes. Remove the toothpicks and transfer the pastries to a serving platter, with the wings facing up.

Flora, Fauna, and Merryweather Fruit Wands

Sleeping Beauty

The three good fairies in *Sleeping Beauty* look after Briar Rose—that's their special name for Aurora—to keep her safe from Maleficent's evil curse. The fairies do love their magic wands, even if the wands can only be used for stirring tea—or making sweet fruit kebabs like these. The trick here is to slice the watermelon thick enough for the stars to stay on the skewers and not crack.

Flora, Fauna, and Merryweather Fruit Wands

GF, V | **Yield:** 8 wands and about ½ cup yogurt dip

FRUIT KEBABS

1 mini watermelon

Assorted fruit such as grapes, small strawberries, and blueberries

Skewers

YOGURT DIP

½ cup vanilla yogurt

1 teaspoon minced fresh mint

Zest of 1 lime

1. **To make the fruit kebabs:** Place the watermelon on a cutting board and slice it through the center. Place one of the cut ends on the cutting board and carefully cut away all the rind. Slice the watermelon into ¾-inch-thick slices. Use a 3- to 4-inch star-shape cookie cutter to cut out 8 stars.

2. One kebab at a time, thread the grapes, strawberries, and blueberries onto a skewer, using 6 to 8 pieces of fruit. Leave half of the skewer free for a handle, and leave enough room at the sharp end for the watermelon stars.

3. Carefully thread the watermelon stars onto the end of each skewer.

4. **To make the yogurt dip:** In a small bowl, stir together the yogurt, mint, and lime zest. Serve with the fruit kebabs for dipping.

Deviled Dragon Eggs

Sleeping Beauty

Maleficent doesn't receive an invite to the christening of infant Princess Aurora, so what is an evil fairy to do? Curse the princess, of course, and transform into an enormous fire-breathing dragon. As such, she rains down terror upon King Stefan's kingdom and is intent on exacting her revenge. These Deviled "Dragon" Eggs may look as terrifying as Maleficent, but they're delicious and impressive.

Deviled Dragon Eggs

GF, V | **Yield:** 24 pieces

8 cups shredded red cabbage
12 large eggs
2 tablespoons olive oil
1 tablespoon mayonnaise
1 teaspoon Dijon mustard
1 teaspoon chopped fresh dill, plus more for garnish
Salt and pepper, to taste

1. Place 4 cups of the shredded cabbage in a medium saucepan. Cover the cabbage so it's totally submerged in water with at least 1 inch of water above it. Boil over medium-high heat until tender and the water is deep purple, 20 to 30 minutes. Using a slotted spoon, remove the cooked shredded cabbage and discard, leaving the water in the pan.

2. While the cabbage is cooking, prepare the eggs. Place the eggs in a separate medium saucepan and cover with water by at least 1 inch. Over medium-high heat, bring the water to a full boil. As soon as the water is boiling, remove the pan from the heat and cover. Let the eggs sit in the hot water for 15 minutes, then remove to an ice bath to chill for 1 minute.

3. Lightly crack the egg shells by rolling them on a kitchen towel on the counter. You want there to be fine cracks, but for the shell to still adhere. The finer the cracks, the better the result will be, so be careful.

4. Place the eggs in a storage container with a lid. Pour the cabbage water over the eggs, cover, and chill for at least 12 hours or overnight.

5. Remove the eggs from the water, then peel the shells. The result should be beautiful purple marbling of the egg whites. Cut each egg in half lengthwise. Scoop out the yolk into a medium mixing bowl, and place the whites on a platter.

6. In the bowl with the yolks, add the olive oil, mayonnaise, mustard, dill, salt, and pepper. Stir to combine, then divide evenly between the cups of the egg whites.

7. Top eggs with a sprinkle of dill and serve eggs over nests made with the remaining raw cabbage. Chill before serving.

Dalmatian Pancakes with Strawberry Compote

One Hundred and One Dalmatians

Cruella de Vil simply cannot live without furs, or so she says. Ever in the pursuit of those puppies as well as high fashion, Cruella races through the countryside—a vision of black, white, and red.

These delicious pancakes are a riff on Dalmatian cookies, with a vivid red strawberry compote that brings to mind the black, white, and red of Cruella's classic look, without any of the evil.

Dalmatian Pancakes
with Strawberry Compote

V | **Yield:** 8 to 10 pancakes

STRAWBERRY COMPOTE
1 pound strawberries
½ cup sugar
Juice of half a lemon
½ teaspoon vanilla bean paste

PANCAKES
1 cup all-purpose flour
2 teaspoons baking powder
½ teaspoon salt
2 tablespoons sugar
1 cup milk
1 egg, beaten
2 tablespoons butter, melted
1 teaspoon vanilla extract
¼ cup white chocolate chips
¼ cup milk chocolate chips
Nonstick cooking spray

1. **To make the strawberry compote:** Wash and chop the strawberries, discarding stems and hulls of the fruit. Combine fruit with remaining ingredients in a medium saucepan. Bring to a boil over medium heat, then reduce to a simmer and cook about 15 minutes, until fruit has softened and sauce has thickened. Remove from heat and set aside to cool.

2. **To make the pancakes:** In a mixing bowl, combine the dry ingredients. Add the wet ingredients, and stir to combine. Let stand 10 minutes.

3. Heat a large skillet over medium heat. Off the burner, spray it with nonstick cooking spray. Drop batter by a ¼-cup measuring cup into pan, being careful not to crowd pancakes.

4. Cook until golden brown and bubbles rise to the surface, about 3 minutes. Flip, and cook another 2 to 3 minutes, until golden brown. Remove from heat and transfer to a plate tented with aluminum foil to keep pancakes warm. Repeat with remaining batter. Serve topped with strawberry compote and, if desired, additional white and milk chocolate chips.

Bare Necessities
Banana Muffins

The Jungle Book

In the jungle, there's no lack of fresh fruit.
And when it comes to fruit, it's bananas for
Baloo and Mowgli. Cooked up in a nice,
warm muffin, these make a perfect breakfast
before a lazy day of floating down the river!

NOTE: These muffins will be large and have tops that
spread out onto the top of the muffin pan. Use a knife
or fork if necessary to remove muffins from the pan
without breaking tops.

Bare Necessities Banana Muffins

V | **Yield:** 12 muffins

STREUSEL
3 tablespoons granulated sugar

3 tablespoons brown sugar

3 tablespoons all-purpose flour

Dash salt

2 tablespoons unsalted butter, melted

2 tablespoons chopped walnuts

MUFFINS
Nonstick cooking spray

2 cups all-purpose flour

1 cup whole wheat flour

2 teaspoons baking powder

½ teaspoon baking soda

½ teaspoon salt

¾ cup granulated sugar

2 large eggs

6 tablespoons unsalted butter, melted

1¼ cups buttermilk

1 ripe banana, mashed

1 teaspoon vanilla extract

½ cup chopped walnuts, toasted

1. **To make the streusel:** Heat the oven to 375°F. Spray a standard 12-cup muffin tin generously with nonstick cooking spray, spraying the top as well as the cups; set aside.

2. In a small bowl, combine the granulated sugar, brown sugar, flour, and salt. Stir in the butter and walnuts; set aside.

3. **To make the muffins:** In a large bowl, stir together the all-purpose flour, whole wheat flour, baking powder, baking soda, salt, and sugar. In a medium bowl, beat the eggs. Whisk in the melted butter, buttermilk, banana, and vanilla.

4. Add the banana mixture to the flour mixture. Fold together gently with a rubber spatula until nearly combined. Stir in the ½ cup walnuts just until combined. (Do not overmix.) Divide the batter evenly among the muffin cups. Sprinkle the streusel over top of the batter.

5. Bake until golden brown and a toothpick inserted into center comes out clean, 20 to 25 minutes. Cool in the pan for 5 minutes. Remove from the pan and serve warm.

Roquefort Blue Cheese Wheels

The Aristocats

As Madame Bonfamille's pets, Marie, Toulouse, and Berlioz have access to the finest foods. And what could be better than sharing a delicious little treat with their good friend Roquefort the Mouse? Cooked up in a puff pastry, this treat is a snack worthy of any Aristocat!

Roquefort Blue Cheese Wheels

V | **Yield:** About 36 pinwheels

4 ounces Roquefort cheese, room temperature
4 ounces cream cheese, room temperature
1 large egg
¼ cup finely chopped green onion
1 teaspoon finely chopped fresh rosemary
½ teaspoon freshly ground black pepper
Half of one 17.3-ounce package
frozen puff pastry, thawed (1 sheet)
1 cup toasted pecans, finely chopped
1 egg yolk, beaten

1. In a medium bowl, combine the Roquefort and cream cheese. Beat with an electric mixer until combined. Beat in the egg. With a rubber spatula, stir in the green onion, rosemary, and pepper.

2. On a lightly floured work surface, unfold the puff pastry and roll out to a 10-by-12-inch rectangle. Spread the cheese mixture evenly over the pastry, leaving a 1-inch border along one of the long edges. Sprinkle the pecans evenly over the cheese mixture.

3. Brush the egg yolk over the 1-inch strip of pastry without filling. Starting at the opposite edge, roll up the pastry tightly into a spiral log. Seal the edge to the log by pressing and pinching. Wrap the log with plastic wrap and chill in the refrigerator for 1 to 2 hours or until very firm.

4. Heat the oven to 400°F. Line a large rimmed baking pan with parchment paper; set aside.

5. Place the chilled log on a cutting board. Cut with a sharp knife into ¼-inch-thick slices. Place slices 1 inch apart on the prepared baking sheet.

6. Bake until golden brown and crispy, 15 to 20 minutes. Serve warm or at room temperature.

Flotsam & Jetsam Party Mix

The Little Mermaid

Flotsam and Jetsam are moray eels, Ursula's "beloved babies" who do her bidding. In the dictionary, flotsam is defined as the wreckage of a shipwreck, and jetsam is anything that has been thrown off a ship and washed up on shore. They're fancy words for bits and pieces of things, like this sweet and savory party mix.

Don't be afraid of the hot sauce in this recipe. The amount called for is mild in the final result. For more of a kick, use up to ½ cup of hot sauce, and add a pinch of cayenne and a bit more sugar to the mixture.

Flotsam & Jetsam Party Mix

Yield: 8 to 10 servings

½ cup (1 stick) butter
2 teaspoons garlic powder
2 teaspoons smoked paprika
2 tablespoons Worcestershire sauce
¼ cup buffalo-style hot sauce
1½ tablespoons brown sugar
2 cups square corn cereal
2 cups square rice cereal
2 cups square cheese crackers
2 cups pretzels
1 cup dried cranberries
1 cup chocolate chips

1. Preheat the oven to 250°F. In a small saucepan over medium heat, melt the butter. Add the garlic powder, smoked paprika, Worcestershire sauce, hot sauce, and brown sugar. Cook for 2 minutes until combined.

2. In a large mixing bowl, combine the corn cereal, rice cereal, crackers, and pretzels. (Omit anything that will melt or won't hold up to baking for this step.) Pour the hot mixture over the contents of the bowl and mix well.

3. Spread the mixture over two lined baking sheets in a single layer. Bake until golden and fragrant, about 45 minutes. Remove from the oven and allow to cool.

4. Mix in the dried fruit and chocolate. Serve.

Hot Hors D'oeuvres Gougères

Beauty and the Beast

The enchanted objects of Beast's castle live to serve, and one of the things they serve Belle are delicious hot hors d'oeuvres. These cheese puffs are a staple at any French dinner table . . . and now they can be one at your table as well!

Hot Hors D'oeuvres Gougères

V | **Yield:** About 40 cheese puffs

1 cup plus 1 tablespoon water
½ cup butter
1 teaspoon salt
1 cup all-purpose flour
Dash nutmeg
Dash freshly ground black pepper
5 large eggs, divided
1 cup shredded Gruyère cheese
Grated Parmesan cheese

1. Preheat the oven to 425°F. Line two large baking sheets with parchment paper.

2. In a large saucepan, combine 1 cup water, butter, and salt. Bring to a boil over medium-high heat. Add the flour all at once along with the nutmeg and pepper. Beat vigorously with a wooden spoon until the dough comes together and pulls away from the sides of pan. Cook and stir 1 minute more. Remove from the heat and let cool 5 minutes.

3. Using a wooden spoon or electric mixer, beat in 4 of the eggs, one at a time. Beat well after each addition until dough is smooth. Stir in the Gruyère cheese.

4. Place the dough in a large pastry bag with a 1-inch round opening. Pipe 1½-inch mounds on prepared baking sheets about 1½ inches apart. If mounds have a sharp peak, pat them down with a wet fingertip.

5. In a small dish, beat together the remaining egg and 1 tablespoon of water. Brush the tops of the dough mounds with the egg mixture; sprinkle with the Parmesan cheese.

6. Bake for 10 minutes. Reduce heat to 375°F and bake until golden brown and the cracks look dry, 20 to 25 minutes. Turn off the oven. Remove the baking sheets from the oven and pierce the puffs with a fork to allow steam to escape. Return to the warm oven and let dry for 10 minutes.

7. Serve hot.

Cave of Wonders Cardamom Breadsticks

Aladdin

Brimming with riches, jewels, and magical items—including the Genie's magic lamp—the Cave of Wonders is a pretty special place. These soft, pillowy breadsticks are pretty special too. Flavored with cardamom, a spice popular in Middle Eastern cooking, they are delightful served with a cup of warm tea.

Cave of Wonders Cardamom Breadsticks

V | **Yield:** 20 breadsticks

1⅓ cups warm water
1½ teaspoons active dry yeast
2 tablespoons sugar
3 cups all-purpose flour
1 teaspoon salt
1 teaspoon cardamom
1 tablespoon unsalted butter, melted
Coarse salt, for sprinkling

1. In a large bowl, combine the water, yeast, and sugar; let stand for 10 minutes or until the yeast foams. Stir the yeast mixture if specks of yeast appear not yet moistened. Add 1½ cups of the flour, the salt, and cardamom to the bowl, then stir to combine. Add the remaining 1½ cups of flour and stir to combine. The dough will be sticky and should pull away from the sides of the bowl. With floured hands, knead dough until smooth, 4 to 5 minutes.

2. Transfer the dough to an extra-large greased bowl. Cover the bowl with a towel. Let the dough rise at least 90 minutes, or until doubled in size.

3. Line a baking sheet with parchment paper. Punch dough down. Evenly divide dough into 20 portions. Roll each portion into a ¾-inch-diameter stick about 8 to 10 inches long. Space breadsticks on prepared baking sheet, allowing 1 inch between each stick. (If necessary, use two baking sheets.) Cover breadsticks with a damp towel and let rise for 1 hour.

4. Preheat the oven to 425°F. Brush the breadsticks with the melted butter and sprinkle with coarse salt. Bake for 10 to 12 minutes, or until golden. Remove the breadsticks from the oven, and transfer to a wire rack to cool slightly.

Flit Berry Pudding Dip

Pocahontas

Pocahontas's hummingbird friend Flit is tiny, just like the berries in this pudding dip. And hummingbirds notoriously love sweet things! Wojapi is the name for a Native American berry sauce that is thickened into a jam-like texture. Though fresh berries are great, this wojapi recipe is just as good if made with frozen berries instead. If using frozen berries, thaw and drain them before starting this recipe. It has a pudding-like texture, and by serving it with fruit cut into crudités, it could double as a dessert.

Flit Berry Pudding Dip

GF*, V | **Yield:** 4 servings

2 cups blueberries
1 cup raspberries
1 cup blackberries
2 tablespoons honey, or more to taste
Sliced fruit or crackers, for serving

1. In a medium-size saucepan over low heat, combine the blueberries, raspberries, blackberries, honey, and ½ cup water. Smash the fruit with a spatula or potato masher to release the juices and help it break down.

2. Cook until the mixture is soft and thickened, about 30 minutes, stirring frequently enough that no bits of fruit stick to the bottom of the pan.

3. Serve warm or chilled alongside sliced fruit or crackers.

NOTE: This is gluten-free if served with fruit, and it's also gluten-free if you serve it with gluten-free crackers, of course.

Tea Eggs

Mulan

To do her best in battle, Mulan needs snacks that will give her energy and help her brain work quickly. Eggs are high in protein and one of the best dietary sources of choline, an important nutrient for brainpower. This exciting version of boiled eggs is made by cracking eggshells before marinating the eggs. If you don't have tamari sauce on hand and can tolerate the gluten in soy sauce, you can substitute an equal amount.

Mulan Tea Eggs

GF, V | **Yield:** 12 eggs

⅓ cup tamari sauce
1 teaspoon five-spice powder
2 teaspoons honey
½ teaspoon salt
2 black tea bags
12 eggs
Salt and black pepper

1. **To make the marinade:** In a medium-size saucepan combine the tamari, five-spice powder, honey, salt, tea bags, and 2½ cups water. Bring to a boil, then reduce heat and simmer for 10 minutes. Strain and set aside to cool.

2. **To cook the eggs:** Place the raw eggs in a medium-size pot and cover with water. Bring to a boil, then reduce to a simmer and cook to your desired level of doneness: 7 minutes for soft- to medium-boiled eggs, or 10 minutes for hard-boiled eggs. Remove the eggs from the water and place them in an ice bath to chill quickly. Once chilled, tap the eggs gently all over with the back of a spoon. You want small cracks all over the surface. Don't tap too hard, or you'll create cracks too large for the design to be prominent.

3. **To marinate the eggs:** Place them in a resealable plastic bag and pour the marinade over them. Seal tightly and marinate in the fridge for 24 hours, turning over after 8 to 12 hours to make sure the marinade permeates all parts of the eggs.

4. **To serve:** Remove the eggs from the marinade and peel off the cracked shells. The eggs should have a marbled appearance, with dark brown coloring from the marinade. Sprinkle with salt and black pepper, if desired.

Mudka's Meat Hut Mug of Meat

The Emperor's New Groove

Kuzco and Pacha are on the run, and there aren't many places to hide. Luckily, they manage to find temporary sanctuary at Mudka's Meat Hut, a local diner known for its specialty: the Mug of Meat! This amazing dish, inspired by the one invented by the diner's owner, Major Mudka, more than fifty years ago, is sure to leave you more than satisfied!

Mudka's Meat Hut Mug of Meat

GF | **Yield:** 1 serving

Vegetable oil, for greasing
4 ounces extra-lean ground beef
1 large egg, beaten
2 tablespoons uncooked instant rice
2 tablespoons ketchup, plus more
for garnish
1 tablespoon chopped black olives,
plus more for garnish
1 tablespoon chopped canned
green chiles
1 tablespoon frozen corn kernels,
plus more for garnish
½ teaspoon smoked paprika
½ teaspoon chile powder
⅛ teaspoon ground cumin
Pinch onion powder
Pinch salt and pepper

1. Grease a large (10- to 12-ounce) microwave-safe mug with vegetable oil.

2. In a medium bowl, combine the beef, egg, rice, ketchup, olives, chiles, corn, paprika, chile powder, cumin, onion powder, and salt and pepper to taste. Mix well with a fork or your hands. Shape into a ball.

3. Place the meat ball into the mug. Press the meat ball down slightly to fill the mug evenly. Cover with vented plastic wrap.

4. Microwave on high for 3 minutes or until no longer pink in center and an instant-read thermometer inserted into the center registers 165°F. Cool 5 minutes before serving.

5. Warm about 1 tablespoon of corn kernels in a microwave-safe cup in the microwave for 5 seconds. Garnish the meatloaf with a squiggle of ketchup, olives, and warmed corn kernels.

Experimental Sweet and Savory Bao Buns

Lilo & Stitch

Dr. Jumba Jookiba is definitely a kooky scientist. In fact, his genetic experiments caused so much chaos that he got banned from his own planet! Perhaps he would have been better off experimenting with recipes, like this tasty spread of dim sum buns. There are two different fillings, one sweet and one spicy—blending an array of delicious island flavors in these fun-to-eat bao buns. It's a fantastic mix without any of the chaos of his other experiments!

Experimental Sweet and Savory Bao Buns

Yield: 10 servings

10 premade bao buns (can be found online), divided

SAVORY BAO BUNS

⅓ cup mayonnaise

⅓ cup Dijon mustard

10 butter lettuce leaves or lettuce cups

1 cup bean sprouts, divided evenly for 5 buns

2 carrots, peeled, sliced, and divided evenly
for 5 buns

1 cup pork chicharrones, divided evenly for 5 buns

5 teaspoons lehua honey (Hawaiian honey made from
lehua blossoms)

SWEET BAO BUNS

1 cup hazelnut spread

2 strawberries per bun,
thinly sliced

25 blueberries

2½ ounces peanut
butter chips, evenly
divided for 5 buns

5 pinches Hawaiian
salt, or kosher salt

Banana leaves or
ti leaves, for serving,
(optional)

1. **To make the savory bao buns:** Take 5 bao buns and spread the inside of the buns evenly with about 1 tablespoon mayonnaise and Dijon mustard.

2. Place the following ingredients inside the buns in this order: 2 pieces of lettuce, 1 ounce of bean sprouts, an even split of carrots, and a chicharron.

3. Then drip about 1 ounce of honey over each bun.

4. **To make the sweet bao buns:** Take the other 5 bao buns and spread evenly with the hazelnut spread.

5. Place the following ingredients inside the buns in this order: 2 sliced strawberries, 5 blueberries, and a few peanut butter chips.

6. Sprinkle the salt evenly over each bun.

7. **To serve:** Line a sushi-style platter with banana or ti leaves, if desired, then place the buns on top.

Big Daddy Beignets

The Princess and the Frog

Tiana may make the best gumbo around, but it's her beignets that really make her stand out. A staple of New Orleans life, Tiana's beignets are made with lots of heart . . . which may be why Charlotte wants her father to buy so many of them for her party. She's hoping one taste will land her the heart of a prince!

Big Daddy Beignets

V | **Yield:** 36 beignets

2¾ to 3¼ cups all-purpose flour, divided

One ¼-ounce package active dry yeast

¼ teaspoon ground nutmeg

1 cup whole milk

¼ cup granulated sugar

2 tablespoons shortening or butter

½ teaspoon salt

1 large egg

Vegetable oil for deep frying, plus more for greasing the bowl

Powdered sugar

Honey

1. In a large mixing bowl, combine 1¼ cups of the flour, the yeast, and nutmeg.

2. In a small saucepan, combine the milk, sugar, shortening, and salt. Heat and stir over medium-low until warm (120°F to 130°F) and the shortening is nearly melted. Add the warm milk mixture and egg to the flour mixture. Beat with an electric mixer on low for 30 seconds to combine, then beat for 3 minutes on high. Stir in enough of the remaining flour with a wooden spoon to make a soft dough.

3. On a lightly floured surface, shape the dough into a ball. Place the dough in a greased bowl, turning once to coat the surface of the dough. Cover and chill the dough in the refrigerator for at least 4 hours or overnight.

4. On a lightly floured surface, roll the dough to an 18-by-12-inch rectangle. Cut the dough into thirty-six 3-by-2-inch rectangles. Cover and let rest for 30 minutes.

5. In a large saucepan or deep fryer, heat 2 inches of oil to 375°F. Place a wire rack on a large baking pan and cover with paper towels. Fry 2 to 3 dough rectangles at a time for about 1 minute, turning once. Remove with a slotted spoon and drain on the paper towels. Return the oil to 375°F and repeat with the remaining dough.

6. Serve warm, dusted generously with powdered sugar and drizzled with honey.

Sweet Potato Pie Muffins

The Princess and the Frog

Sweet potato pie is a Southern classic you might find at Tiana's Palace. Here, sweet potato pie is reimagined as muffins instead. These vegan muffins are so delicious, you won't notice they have no added oil or butter. They're a filling breakfast that tastes like an indulgent dessert.

Sweet Potato Pie Muffins

V+ | **Yield:** 12 muffins

1½ cups whole wheat flour
½ cup coconut sugar
1 teaspoon baking powder
½ teaspoon baking soda
½ teaspoon salt
1½ teaspoons pumpkin pie spice
2 cups sweet potatoes, cooked and mashed
¾ cup almond or oat milk
2 tablespoons pure maple syrup
1 tablespoon apple cider vinegar
½ teaspoon vanilla extract

1. Preheat the oven to 375°F. Grease or spray a 12-cup muffin pan with cooking spray.

2. In a large mixing bowl, whisk together the flour, coconut sugar, baking powder, baking soda, salt, and pumpkin pie spice. Make a well with the whisk in the center of the ingredients, and add the sweet potatoes, milk, maple syrup, vinegar, and vanilla. Use a spatula to fold the ingredients together until combined.

3. Divide the batter among the prepared muffin-pan cups. Bake until golden, about 20 minutes.

Almond Bear Claw Biscuits

Brave

Basic baking powder biscuits get a punch
of flavor and paw-like flair in this almond-
scented recipe. As a tribute to the moment
when Merida reaches for her mother's paw
and is saved from the claws of Mor'du, these
cute biscuits will be a teatime highlight.

Almond Bear Claw Biscuits

V | **Yield:** 8 biscuits

1 cup all-purpose flour
½ teaspoon salt
2 teaspoons baking powder
2 tablespoons cold unsalted butter, cut into 8 pieces
¼ cup plus 2 tablespoons milk
1 teaspoon almond extract
40 almond slices
1 egg white, beaten

1. Preheat the oven to 350°F. Line a large baking sheet with parchment paper.

2. In a large bowl, sift together the flour, salt, and baking powder. Add the butter to the bowl. Using a pastry cutter or two knives, cut the butter into the flour mixture until it resembles coarse crumbs. Add the milk and almond extract, and stir to mix. The dough will be crumbly.

3. Turn the dough out onto a floured cutting board. Using clean, floured hands, knead the dough lightly until a cohesive ball forms. Use a floured rolling pin to roll the dough to ½-inch thickness.

4. Cut the dough into 2-inch rounds with a biscuit cutter, gathering and rerolling dough to form a total of 8 biscuits.

5. Place the biscuits on the prepared baking sheet. Press 5 almond slices into the top edge of each biscuit, forming the "bear nails." Brush the biscuits with the egg white. Bake for 15 to 17 minutes, until golden brown. Enjoy hot from the oven.

6. Extra biscuits can be stored at room temperature in an airtight container for up to 2 days.

Scottish Cranachan

Brave

Merida needs all the energy she can muster for her sportsmanship, and breakfast is the perfect place to start. Cranachan is a beloved Scottish dessert, but here it gets a healthful makeover fit for breakfast. Since Scottish oats aren't easily available in America, the same style can be acquired by briefly pulsing oats in a blender or a food processor. We're also using whipped yogurt rather than pure whipped cream, and lots of raspberry goodness layered in.

Scottish Cranachan

GF, V | **Yield:** 4 servings

OATMEAL
2 cups old-fashioned rolled oats, pulsed briefly
several times in a blender or food processor

½ teaspoon salt

2 tablespoons pure maple syrup

RASPBERRY SAUCE
2 cups raspberries, fresh
or thawed if frozen

1 tablespoon honey

WHIPPED YOGURT
½ cup whipping cream

2 cups raspberry or
strawberry Greek yogurt

1. **To make the oatmeal:** Add oats, 4 cups water, salt, and maple syrup to a medium saucepan; cook per package instructions.

2. **To make the raspberry sauce:** In a small saucepan combine raspberries, honey, and 3 tablespoons water. Cook over medium heat, mashing occasionally, until raspberries are broken down, about 10 minutes. Remove from the heat and let cool slightly. Use an immersion blender to blend the sauce until smooth. (Or pour the sauce into the bowl of a food processor fitted with a steel blade and process until smooth.) Strain the sauce through a fine-mesh strainer into a bowl. Refrigerate the sauce, uncovered, until ready to assemble.

3. **To make the whipped yogurt:** Whip the whipping cream with an electric mixer until stiff peaks form. Slowly fold in the yogurt, then slowly fold in ¼ cup of the raspberry sauce.

4. **To assemble:** Layer the oatmeal, raspberry sauce, and whipped yogurt in one large bowl or four single-serving dishes until all ingredients are used, ending with whipped yogurt on top.

Heart of Te Fiti Spinach-Artichoke-Mozzarella Pinwheels

Moana

Moana sails away on a voyage to return the Heart of Te Fiti to its rightful place and restore balance to the world. These little pinwheels, filled with spinach, artichokes, and mozzarella, are meant to be symbols of the mythical heart.

Heart of Te Fiti Spinach-Artichoke-Mozzarella Pinwheels

V | **Yield:** 8 pinwheels

1 sheet puff pastry, thawed
½ cup ricotta cheese
1 cup baby spinach
2 cloves garlic, minced
¼ teaspoon salt
⅛ teaspoon freshly ground black pepper
½ cup chopped canned artichoke hearts, drained well
1 cup shredded mozzarella cheese

1. Preheat the oven to 350°F. Line a large baking sheet with parchment paper.

2. Lay the puff pastry on a lightly floured cutting board.

3. In the bowl of a food processor or blender, combine the ricotta cheese, spinach, garlic, salt, and pepper. Process until well combined (the mixture should be green). Spread the ricotta mixture on the puff pastry. Sprinkle the pastry and ricotta mixture with the artichoke hearts and mozzarella cheese, then roll the pastry into a log. Place the log in the freezer for 20 to 30 minutes to firm up.

4. Use a sharp knife to cut the rolled-up pastry into ¾-inch pieces. Place each slice on the baking sheet, gently reshaping into a round if necessary.

5. Bake for 22 to 24 minutes, or until the tops are golden brown. Remove the pinwheels from the oven and cool on a wire rack for 10 minutes before transferring to a serving platter. Enjoy warm.

Elote Callejero

Coco

Movie-goers think of popcorn as a go-to movie snack, but if you're going to watch *Coco*, why not instead prepare this delicious, iconic Mexican street food made of corn? It gets its kick from a flavorful dressing, which you can mix up while you're grilling your ears of corn. You could almost say that the spicy dressing will bring music to your ears (of corn!) while you are watching the music-filled *Coco*.

Elote Callejero

GF, V | **Yield:** 4 servings

4 ears fresh corn, shucked

1 tablespoon vegetable oil

1 teaspoon kosher salt

¼ cup Mexican crema

¼ cup mayonnaise

½ lime, zest and juice

1 garlic clove, grated

½ cup Cotija cheese,
finely crumbled,
plus more for garnish

¼ cup cilantro, leaves and
stems finely chopped,
plus more for garnish

1 teaspoon cayenne chile powder

Hot sauce of your choice,
for garnishing

Lime wedges,
for garnishing

1. Preheat an outdoor grill or grill pan to medium heat. With clean hands or a brush, rub each ear of corn in the vegetable oil and a generous pinch of salt. Place the corn on the grill and cook until it is evenly charred on all sides, about 10 minutes.

2. While the corn is cooking, mix together in a large mixing bowl the crema, mayonnaise, lime zest and juice, grated garlic, Cotija cheese, cilantro, and chile powder. When the corn is finished cooking, remove it from the grill; roll each cob in the crema-and-cheese mixture, and then transfer it to a platter. Garnish to taste with the remaining cheese, cilantro, and hot sauce, and serve with a lime wedge.

Mexican Chocolate Popcorn

Coco

Popcorn and chocolate are ancient foods that can be traced back thousands of years to present-day Mexico. Lightly spiced with cinnamon and almond to conjure the flavors of Mexican chocolate, this addictive snack goes perfectly with the talent competition in La Plaza Santa Cecilia in the film, the Sunrise Spectacular, or a cozy movie night at home.

Mexican Chocolate Popcorn

GF, V | **Yield:** 7 cups popcorn

4 tablespoons unsalted butter, plus more for greasing

7 cups freshly popped popcorn

⅓ cup light corn syrup

1 cup sugar

¼ teaspoon kosher salt

3 ounces 72% dark chocolate, finely chopped

¼ teaspoon ground cinnamon

1 teaspoon almond extract

¾ teaspoon baking soda

1. Move the oven rack to the middle position, and preheat the oven to 250°F. Line a baking sheet with aluminum foil, and grease with butter or oil spray.

2. Place the freshly popped popcorn in a large mixing bowl, and set aside.

3. To a large pan, add the butter, corn syrup, sugar, salt, and ⅓ cup water. Bring to a boil over high heat. Reduce heat to medium-low, and cook, stirring constantly, with a rubber spatula until the sugar dissolves and the mixture is smooth, 3 to 5 minutes.

4. Turn off the heat. Stir in the chocolate, cinnamon, and almond extract until the chocolate is melted; then immediately add the baking soda. When the chocolate sauce is foamy, pour it over the popcorn and quickly coat the popcorn.

5. Scrape the popcorn onto the prepared baking sheet, and level it with the spatula in an even single layer. Bake the popcorn for 20 minutes; remove the pan and carefully stir the popcorn.

6. Level the popcorn again in an even single layer; then put it back in the oven to continue baking for another 30 minutes until the chocolate coating forms a crispy shell.

7. Remove the popcorn from the oven and stir one more time. Let it cool completely in the pan before serving.

Uno, Dos, Tres Avocado Spread

Encanto

Abuela's candle gave her family a miracle. It also feels like a miracle how this silky and smooth Ají de aguacate stays green for a long time! What helps this Uno, Dos, Tres Avocado Spread to preserve its vibrant color? The magical key is the avocado's pit sitting in the middle of the tightly sealed container, protecting the spread's texture from oxidation and maintaining its bright green color for a long time.

Uno, Dos, Tres Avocado Spread

GF, V, V+* | **Yield:** 2½ cups

¼ cup white vinegar

2 tablespoons lemon juice

½ teaspoon salt

½ teaspoon freshly ground black pepper

1½ cups finely diced avocado
(about 1 avocado) (save the pit)

1 cup chopped and seeded tomatoes
(about 2 tomatoes)

¼ cup finely diced red onion
(about ¼ large onion)

¼ cup chopped scallions
(about ½ scallion, green part included)

¼ cup seeded ají dulce, minced
(about 5 sweet red peppers)

¼ cup chopped cilantro

½ teaspoon minced and seeded
habanero pepper (optional)

2 hard-boiled eggs, peeled and
finely chopped (optional)

1. In a blender, add the vinegar, lemon juice, salt, and black pepper and blend for about 1 minute. Add the avocado and blend to a smooth consistency, about 2 minutes.

2. Pour into a medium bowl, add the tomatoes, red onion, scallions, ají dulce, cilantro, and habanero pepper, if using. Add the hard-boiled eggs, if using, mix with a fork, and serve. Some egg can be placed on top as decoration. To keep from browning, add the avocado pit to the mixture, cover, and refrigerate until ready to use.

3. Serve with tortilla chips or raw vegetable crudités, such as carrots, cucumbers, and broccoli.

NOTE: This recipe is vegan if the eggs are omitted. It will last up to 2 days in the refrigerator without the egg.

Guava and Cheese Mini Bites

Encanto

These sweet mini bites are called *casado* or *matrimonio*, meaning wed or wedding. A chunk of guava paste and a thick slice of white cheese are married to create this quick Colombian dessert called *Bocadillo con queso*.

They're widely known in all regions of Colombia and would surely be a favorite of Mariano Guzmán, who has so much love inside—especially for these!

Guava and Cheese Mini Bites

GF, V | **Yield:** 3 servings

1 pound white farmer cheese
1 pound guava paste, or guava squares

SPECIALTY TOOLS
Decorative toothpicks

1. Slice the cheese and guava
   paste into ½-by-½-inch
   squares. Pin one on top of
   the other with decorative
   toothpicks and serve.

FIND MORE RECIPES FROM Disney

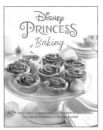

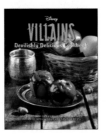

INSIGHT
EDITIONS

PO Box 3088
San Rafael, CA 94912
www.insighteditions.com

Find us on Facebook:
www.facebook.com/InsightEditions

Follow us on Instagram:
@insighteditions

Based on the book *The Hundred and
One Dalmatians* by Dodie Smith
Published by Viking Press

The Aristocats is based on the book
by Thomas Rowe.

ISBN: 979-8-88663-699-4

Publisher: Raoul Goff
Group Publisher & SVP: Vanessa Lopez
VP, Creative: Chrissy Kwasnik
VP, Manufacturing: Alix Nicholaeff
Editorial Director: Paul Ruditis
Art Director: Stuart Smith
Senior Designer: Judy Wiatrek Trum
Editor: Jennifer Pellman
Executive Project Editor: Maria Spano
Production Manager: Deena Hashem
Senior Production Manager, Subsidiary
Rights: Lina s Palma-Temena

  REPLANTED PAPER

Insight Editions, in association with Roots of Peace,
will plant two trees for each tree used in the
manufacturing of this book. Roots of Peace is an
internationally renowned humanitarian organization
dedicated to eradicating land mines worldwide and
converting war-torn lands into productive farms
and wildlife habitats. Roots of Peace will plant two
million fruit and nut trees in Afghanistan and provide
farmers there with the skills and support necessary
for sustainable land use.

Manufactured in China by Insight Editions
10 9 8 7 6 5 4 3 2 1

Recipe Sources

Pages 9, 29, 57, 85, 93 .... *Disney Princess Tea Parties Cookbook*
by Sarah Walker Caron

Pages 13, 17, 41, 45, 53, 69, 77.... *Disney: Cooking with Magic* by Lisa Kingsley,
Jennifer Peterson, and Brooke Vitale

Pages 21, 25 .... *Alice in Wonderland: The Official Cookbook*
by Elena P. Craig and S. T. Bende

Pages 33, 37, 49 .... *Disney Villains: Devilishly Delicious Cookbook*
by Julie Tremaine

Pages 61, 65, 81, 89 .... *Disney Princess Healthy Treats Cookbook* by Ariane Resnick

Page 73 .... *Lilo and Stitch: The Official Cookbook* by Tim Rita

Pages 97, 101 .... *Coco: The Official Cookbook* by Gino Garcia

Pages 105, 109 .... *Encanto: The Official Cookbook*
by Patricia McCausland-Gallo and Susana Illera Martínez